Activities for **3-5** year olds

Pets

 Brilliant Publications Sue Pearce & Caroline Quin

We hope you enjoy using this book. If you would like further information on other titles published by Brilliant Publications, please write to the address given below.

For further ideas on teaching preschool children about animal welfare contact the RSPCA Education Department, Causeway, Horsham, West Sussex RH12 1HG. Or you could join Partners in Animal Welfare (PAW), the RSPCA's network for teachers and educationalists. Membership of PAW is free and offers: an information pack, termly newsletter packed with teaching ideas, competitions, discounts on resources and news about events in your area.

Note: to avoid the clumsy 'he/she', the child is referred to throughout as 'he'.

Published by Brilliant Publications, The Old School Yard, Leighton Road, Northall,
Dunstable, Bedfordshire LU6 2HA

Written by Sue Pearce and Caroline Quin
Illustrated by Claire Boyce

Printed in Malta by Interprint Limited

© Sue Pearce and Caroline Quin
ISBN 1 897675 38 0

The Publisher accepts no responsibility for accidents arising from the activities described in this book.

First published in 1998
10 9 8 7 6 5 4 3 2 1

Contents

Introduction

Keeping small pet animals in the preschool will help children, particularly those unable to keep pets at home, to:
- learn to respect living and growing things;
- explore and recognize features of animals;
- learn to care for them;
- learn what different species need by way of food, water and habitat.

A pets topic fits in nicely with QCA's Desirable Learning Outcomes, especially in the area of Knowledge and Understanding of the World, as it enables children to explore, recognize and describe features of living things and to communicate their findings in simple ways.

When keeping pets, you will need to make sure that:
- there is a member of staff personally responsible for the welfare of the animals;
- you can provide a suitable environment (contact RSPCA Education Department for advice);
- you can provide suitable housing, food, drink, cleansing and veterinary care at all times, including weekends and holidays;
- you can afford to keep the animals and meet any veterinary fees;
- contact between animals and children is supervised and controlled at all times;
- the animals get adequate rest, away from disturbance;
- the animals are prevented from indiscriminate breeding;
- the animals will not pose health and safety problems such as animal-borne diseases, allergies or injury to the children;
- you comply with current legislation including the Protection of Animals Act 1911 (1912 in Scotland) and the Wildlife and Countryside Act 1981.

Where it is not possible to have small pet animals in the preschool, alternative approaches to providing the children with the opportunity to observe animals could be to:
- observe animals in the garden or nearby park;
- encourage small animals into the garden by providing appropriate habitats; observe how many different minibeasts are in that area, being careful not to disturb or destroy habitats in doing so;
- use videos, slides, CD-ROMs, posters and models.

I went for a walk one morning

What children should learn

Language and literacy – to listen and respond to an action rhyme and to use their imagination.

What you need

Room to move around freely; to be familiar with the structure of the following rhyme:

> I went for a walk one morning and what did I see?
> *(walk around)*
> I saw a big or small … who was looking at me.
> *(stand still and look around)*
> I said 'Good morning'. What do you think he'd say?
> *(keep standing still)*
> (Make noise of animal.) You're right! – he did!
> And then he (ran/flew) away.
> *(Say lines, then continue walking, going back to first line)*

Activity

Encourage the children to suggest animals and to make the appropriate sounds. These could be popular pets (eg a dog), or more unusual ones (eg a bear).

Extension

Ask the children what animals they might see if they went for a real walk. Make a note of their suggestions. Take small groups of children out for a walk. Look for any animals on the way, using the list to mark off any animals the group sees. When you get back to the classroom use the list to remind the children which animals they saw.

Talk about

What noise does the animal make? How does it move? How does it walk, run, etc?

Which pet is yours?

What children should learn

Language and literacy – to take part in a group discussion about their own pets, those of friends and relations, or pets they would like to have.

What you need

Photographs of children's own pets (where possible); pictures of pets from magazines, posters, etc; word cards, printed clearly in lower case: 'cat', 'dog', etc.

Activity

Working in small groups ask the children to show pictures of their own pets and talk about them. Ask, for example: 'What's your pet's name? What does it like to eat? What colour is it?', etc. If a child does not have a pet ask him to pick out a picture from the pile and to talk about it in a similar way. Encourage the children to ask questions of one another, such as: 'Is that the only pet you have?' 'Does your granny / aunty / next door neighbour have a pet?' 'If you had a dog, would you prefer a big one or a little one? Why?'

Extension

Let the children sort the magazine pictures into groups, eg cats, dogs, etc. Stick the groups of pictures on sugar paper, and use the word cards to label the pictures.

Talk about

Does anyone have an unusual pet, such as a snake, or a lizard?

My grandma's cat

What children should learn

Language and literacy – to use adjectives to describe cats and other animals.

What you need

No special equipment.

Activity

Work with a small group of children. Say the line: 'My grandma's cat is a … cat.' Ask the children to add suggestions about their 'grandma's cat'. Encourage them to repeat the whole sentence each time. You could vary the activity by asking the children to suggest more exotic pets that their grandma might own. Ask the children to suggest words to describe those animals.

Extension

As the children get more confident the game can be played using the alphabet. For example: 'My grandma's cat is an **a**ttractive cat'; 'My grandma's cat is a **b**eautiful cat', and so on.

Talk about

Experiment with words and decide whether all the words that have been used to describe a cat could describe another animal, such as a camel. Ask if they have a grandmother and whether she really has a pet. Suggest that some old people like pets for companionship.

Pet stories

What children should learn

Language and literacy – to listen and respond to a story.

What you need

No special equipment.

Activity

Story telling without books is an important skill as it allows the teller to adjust the story to suit the situation. Discuss the basic plot of the story with the children beforehand. Find out if they have any pets or would like to own one.

Tell a story about a pet. Perhaps it is a surprise pet that a child has been longing for. Perhaps it is an expected pet, like a baby kitten, which is not ready to leave its mother yet. Perhaps it is a pet belonging to someone else and the child is asked to look after it. Bring the children into the story by name, eg 'Gemma was going to see a kitten that she would be able to bring home when it was old enough.' Miss out words, or hesitate occasionally, to encourage the children to join in.

Extension

Ask questions about the story to check the children's understanding. If appropriate, produce props such as a collar and lead, a brush, or a pet toy. Talk about the grooming of pets.

Talk about

Ask the children to contribute ideas to the story – 'Gemma is going to choose her kitten. What could she call it? Where would it sleep?'

Rhymes, rhymes, rhymes

What children should learn

Language and literacy – to rhyme and experiment with words.

What you need

List of types of pets: eg cat, kitten, dog, puppy; list of pets' names or potential names: eg Spot, Rover, Felix, Lucky, Snowball, Tinker.

Activity

Give the children an example of a rhyme, eg cat/fat. Ask them to try to find something similar. Ask them to try to rhyme the names of their pets with another word, eg Lucky/mucky. Extend the activity by making up more lengthy rhymes, such as 'The fat cat sat on the mat', with the help of the children. If the children can't think of a real word that rhymes, they could make one up.

Extension

Find suitable pictures and write the rhymes under them. Display the pictures.

Talk about

Talk about how rhymes occur everywhere. (Accept that sometimes rude words will come in as swift rhyming often leads to this.) Adopt the catch phrase 'You're a poet and you didn't know it.' Can you make rhymes for more unusual pets, like a stick insect?

Matching pets

What children should learn

Language and literacy – to match silhouettes, thus helping to develop shape recognition.

What you need

Pictures of pets (cats, dogs, budgies, etc); exactly the same pictures in silhouette. (It may take some time to prepare the pictures, but it is worth it as the game can be played time and time again.) Stick the pictures on to card and cover with clear self-adhesive film.

Activity

Work with a small group of children. Spread the complete pictures on the table. Hold the silhouettes and deal them out to the children, one each. Ask the children to match their silhouette to the appropriate picture. As the children become more proficient, make new cards where the differences between the pets are less obvious. For example, you could have two rabbits, one with both ears sticking straight up, the other with one ear up and the other folded down. Encourage the children to focus on the detail.

Extension

Leave the game out on the table and allow the children to play with it by themselves.

Talk about

Talk about how the shapes match and where the similarities and differences lie. What clues do they look for?

Tortoise drive

What children should learn

Mathematics – to recognize and count numbers one to six.

What you need

One tortoise game card per player (A5 piece of card, with the illustration shown below, covered with clear self-adhesive film); a number die; six large counters and 21 small counters for each player; small dishes to place counters in.

Activity

Work with groups of four to six children (use a smaller group size with younger children and only large counters). Each player has a tortoise card and a dish of counters. The first player throws the die. The player finds the number thrown on his card and covers it using a large counter. Players take turns to throw the die until all the numbered parts of the tortoise have been covered. If a player throws a number he has already covered, then he passes the die on to the next player.

Extension

This game can be extended by using the small counters. Instead of covering the number with a large counter, the child places the corresponding number of small counters on the table beside the tortoise card.

Talk about

Talk about tortoises as pets. Does anyone have one? Has anyone ever seen one, touched one? What was it like? What do tortoises eat? Do they move fast or slow? You could also talk about how tortoises hibernate – some tortoises bury themselves in the same place in the garden each year.

Sizing them up or down

What children should learn

Mathematics – to sort the picture cards into the different type groups and then each group into size.

What you need

Paper; stiff card; photocopier; scissors; clear self-adhesive film.

Before doing the activity you will need to prepare the cards. On a sheet of paper make simple drawings of four to six pet animals (eg gerbil, cat, dog, guinea pig, fish, parakeet). They should be no more than 7 cm x 7 cm each. Photocopy the sheet once in this size, then photocopy it again four or five times more, remembering each time to gradually reduce the size of the photocopy. Cut the pictures out and mount them onto pieces of stiff card. Each card must be the same size – approximately 9 cm x 9 cm. Cover each card with clear self-adhesive film. You should end up with five (or more) cards of each pet animal whose size gradually ranges from 7 cm x 7 cm down to about 2 cm x 2 cm.

Activity

Put all the cards in a pile in the centre of the table. Get the children to sort them into 'pet' piles and then each child can sort his pile again into graduating sizes.

Extension

Children could re-sort cards into same size pet groups.

Talk about

Talk about how things can be of the same type, but very different in size. Look around the room and see what is the same type but of different size, eg tables, chairs, windows, children, adults, books, etc.

Pets' needs

What children should learn

Mathematics – to develop sorting and matching skills.

What you need

Silhouettes of pet animals (you could use the same ones as for *Matching pets*, page 10) mounted on A4 card (one per card); smaller pictures of equipment and food which are generally provided for/required by each type of pet animal (also mounted on card).

Activity

Work with a small group of children. Give them two or three silhouette pictures and a tray of assorted cut-out pictures. The children should sort these and work out which food and equipment belong with each silhouette picture.

Extension

Talk about the suitability of 'swapping' equipment and foods. How would the pet animal manage? Have some examples of some of the pet food/equipment for the children to see and handle where appropriate.

Talk about

What type of food does each type of animal eat? How does their food compare to what we eat? What about their equipment?

Who has a pet?

What children should learn

Personal and social development – to explore people's different needs and desires.

What you need

Some pictures of pets.

Activity

Talk to the children about who has, and who does not have, a pet. Talk about the reasons why people keep pets. Ask why some people cannot have a pet: maybe someone in the family is allergic to animal fur; perhaps they live in a flat which would be unsuitable for pets; perhaps most of the family are out all day so the pet would get very lonely; perhaps the food for the pet would cost too much money.

Extension

Ask the children if they care personally for their own pets. Do they feed the cat, clean out the rabbit hutch, or take the dog for a walk? Do they always do it or only when they feel like it? Who does those jobs if they don't?

Talk about

Since this is a discussion activity the talk can go in many directions. Talk also about why some people find comfort from their pets. Perhaps they are all alone and their pet is their best friend. Perhaps they like stroking their pet and the pet is always nice to them.

Who will mind the pet?

What children should learn

Personal and social development – to understand that pets should be treated with care, respect and concern.

What you need

A large piece of paper or card; some felt-tipped pens; a prepared list of dates; a list of jobs; a list of the children's names.

Activity

Working with a small group of children, draw up a list of tasks that involve the class or playgroup pet. For example: buying food, feeding, cleaning out (maybe grooming if necessary), taking it home at weekends, and taking it home at holiday time. Make a rota chart with the advice, suggestions and help of the children. Ensure that only children who have permission from their parents are assigned to take the pet home. Those who are not so assigned could be allocated other care tasks in the classroom.

Extension

Having made the chart with a small group of children, show it to the whole class. Make a slot at the bottom of the chart to take a card showing the day / date / weekend / holiday dates and showing whose job it is to take care of the pet on any given occasion. Share the task of changing the name of the person responsible for the pet with the whole class every day.

Talk about

Talk about the importance of proper care. Ask the children what would happen if the pets were not cared for properly. Show that a pet is a responsibility as well as a friend. You could bring in how 'relatives' of the pets look after themselves in the wild.

Mix or match

What children should learn

Creative development – to experiment with different animal forms.

What you need

Bold outline drawings of common pets divided into four sections: head, body, legs, tail (draw the lines on the sheet first, then add the details to fit – try to make it so the parts from the different animals are interchangeable); photocopier; paper; four shallow trays; PVA glue; brushes or spreaders; black or dark paper.

Activity

Photocopy several copies of the pet outlines. Cut them up in advance and put each type of body part in a separate shallow tray. Allow the children to choose one piece from each tray (ie one body, legs, head and tail) and stick them together on a sheet of paper to create a 'new' pet. Alternatively, they could try to match the sections to re-form the pet.

Extension

Talk about how you could take parts or features of one thing in order to create something new or more useful.

Talk about

How would animals look if you swapped body parts around, eg an elephant's nose on a budgie. What problems could the new-look birds/animals encounter?

This page may be photocopied and the illustrations enlarged.

I can paint a ...

What children should learn

Creative development – to select and mix colours to create a painted picture of their pet.

What you need

Paint pots containing the most common colours of pets; spare pots (if colour mixing is needed); photograph of child's pet; pet pictures taken from magazines; paint brushes; large sheets of paper; easel; Blu-tack; protective clothing; templates of animals.

Activity

Use the Blu-tack to fasten the child's photograph (or chosen magazine picture) to the corner of the easel. Depending on age/stage, children can 'free' paint their picture, or large templates could be available for the child to draw around and then paint in. If the correct shade is not available you could help the children to mix the paints together to create the right colour for their pet.

Extension

Display the pictures on the wall. You could group the pictures by colour or type. Label the paintings with the child's name and that of the pet.

Talk about

What colour is your pet? Is it the same colour all over? What colour ears does it have? What colour legs?, etc.

Snail trail

What children should learn

Creative development – to create a 'snail trail', using paints and crayons.

What you need

Plain white thick paper or thin card; white crayons or white household-type candles; paint wash (any colours); flat brushes (small household brushes are lovely to use for this); snails or pictures of snails and their trails; protective clothing.

Activity

This activity could be done in conjunction with *Snailarium* (page 29). Work with one or two children at a time. Show them pictures of trails made by snails or let them observe an actual snail's trail. Tell them that they are going to make their own 'snail trail' pictures. Get the children to draw lines on to white paper/card with the white crayons or candles (they may need to apply a little pressure). When they brush paint wash over the whole sheet they will reveal their white snail trails!

Extension

Children could be encouraged to follow the trails with their index fingers. This will promote eye–hand co-ordination and control, and aid concentration. Children could draw a snail on to the paper when the painting is dry.

Talk about

Talk about how fast a snail or slug moves. How long do they think it would take a snail to make the trails on the paper?

Stick a goldfish

What children should learn

Creative development – to make a collage of a goldfish.

What you need

Goldfish shapes of different sizes, cut out of stiff paper or card; lots of shiny and/or bright bits to stick on the fish: gold paper, sequins, orange-coloured tissue, orange felt, etc; PVA glue; spreaders; containers for the glue and for the collage items.

Activity

If possible, look at real goldfish or those in books. Arrange the collage items attractively on the table. Invite the children to 'stick a goldfish'. Let them stick as many of whatever size they like.

Allow the child to concentrate on his composition and complete it in his own way. He may make a goldfish that is hardly recognizable (he may be in his impressionist period!). Afterwards ask him to tell you about his fish.

Extension

Suspend different-sized fish in boxes on black thread to make your own aquarium. Let the children paint the inside and the outside of the boxes.

Talk about

Where do goldfish live (eg in ponds, in tanks and in bowls)? Are all goldfish gold? (Some have patches on them and some are almost white.) Have the children ever seen golden carp? They look like huge goldfish.

Sounds like our pets

What children should learn

Creative development – to move like a pet animal.

What you need

No special equipment.

Activity

Ask the children to stand very still, listen and watch. When you make the sound of a certain pet animal (eg bark like a dog) or a 'face' like a certain animal (eg twitch your nose like a rabbit) ask them to move around like that animal. A good way of getting them to stop, ready for the next animal, is to stand very quiet and still yourself.

Extension

Encourage the children to imitate more exotic pets, eg a snake, spider or parrot.

Talk about

How do pets move? Do they run on four legs? Do they hop, jump or fly? Do they have a ball or wheel to move around in?

Rubbings of our pets

What children should learn

Physical development – small muscle control (this activity requires considerable manual dexterity to hold the paper flat across the template with one hand and rub or scribble with the crayon in the other; less dextrous children may need some help).

What you need

Templates of pets (available from Galt, or make your own from card); white A4 paper; thick crayons (with paper removed); sharp pencils.

Activity

Show the child how to hold the paper across the template with one hand and the crayon flat in the other. The child should rub the crayon across the paper. A 'shadow' picture should result from the template under the paper.

Extension

Using very sharp pencils, have the children draw round the templates. Again, less dextrous children may need some help to succeed with this.

Talk about

Discuss how difficult it is to hold the template and the crayon at the same time. Talk about how the child is succeeding with this and (if necessary) how you might be able to help.

Aunty Flo had a ...

What children should learn

Physical development – to control and co-ordinate their body movements and to use their imagination.

What you need

Space for movement.

Activity

Teach the children the words of the song, to the tune of *Old McDonald Had a Farm*:

> Aunty Flo lived in a bus
> E – I – E – I – O
> and in that bus she kept a …

Encourage the children to choose pet animals for Aunty Flo and to suggest appropriate actions for each one. Ask, for example: 'How do dogs walk? How do they run?'

Extension

Encourage the children to suggest appropriate noises as well. Ask the children how large their chosen pet is. If it is large, exaggerate the noises and actions. If it is small, make small actions and very quiet noises.

Talk about

If Aunty Flo lived in different places, such as in the jungle or under the sea, what different types of 'pets' might she have? For example, if Aunty Flo lived in a tiny house like a doll's house, what would she have room for? The children will need to think about and name tiny creatures / insects.

Pretending to be a ...

What children should learn

Physical development – to develop balance and co-ordination and to improve their gross motor skills.

What you need

Large clear area; some large apparatus, to include: a wooden ladder and safety mats, crash/floor mats, free-standing hoops, tunnels, balls, etc.

Activity

Depending on the number of children and the equipment available, set up different activity areas, to encourage children to move like pets. For example, you might have:

- hamsters – tunnel
- fish or snakes – slithering on floor mats
- budgies – climbing up/down the ladder
- cats – playing with a ball
- dogs – jumping through hoops

Divide the children into groups. At each area the children pretend to be that animal and move in the appropriate way. Rotate the groups between areas.

Extension

Encourage the children to make the noise and/or behave like the relevant pet when at the activity area.

Talk about

What was it like pretending to be the pets – making noises, moving like them? If they could be one of those pets which one would they like to be? Encourage the children to say why.

Who am I?

What children should learn

Knowledge and understanding of the world – to identify each pet animal from a description only.

What you need

A4 size picture cards of six to eight pet animals (as life size as possible for small animals); prepared descriptions or clues of each pet broken down into small sections (don't make them too obvious).

Activity

Sit in a small group with a maximum of three or four children. Hold the cards so that the children can't see the pictures. Tell them you are going to describe one of the pets, giving clues. The child who guesses correctly holds that picture or places it on the floor in front of him until the end of the game. If it looks as though one or two children are getting the correct answer more quickly than the others in the group, then change the system by going round each child so that they all have a chance to answer.

Extension

At the end of the game, sort the pictures into sizes or types, etc. Talk about the baby pet animals' names, the differences between one newborn pet animal and another newborn. Knowledge of length of pregnancies might be useful!

Talk about

Discuss how some animals in the wild are distantly related to our pet animals. Can the children suggest some?

Spot the difference

What children should learn

Knowledge and understanding of the world – to look closely at drawings in order to identify differences.

What you need

Paper; pencil; stiff card; photocopier; correcting fluid; clear self-adhesive film; scissors; water-based pens.

Activity

Do a line drawing of a pet on a sheet of paper. Make two photocopies of it. Keep one copy as it is. Make some changes to the other copy (eg, if it is a dog, draw on a collar or erase his tail with correcting fluid). Photocopy this drawing again to keep the same appearance as the other one. Mount the drawings side by side on to card and cover with clear self-adhesive film. Repeat the same process with other types of pets.

Give each child a card and a water-based pen. Ask him to look for differences and mark ones he spots with the pen. (Wipe the card off afterwards with a damp cloth so that it is ready for the next child.)

Extension

The cards could be made more complex by using more detailed drawings or by increasing the number of details which the child has to find. The size of the cards may need to be increased.

Talk about

Look for and talk about similarities and differences between objects in the room. What differences can the children spot?

A pet with a difference

What children should learn

Knowledge and understanding of the world – to know that farm animals can be pets and that where you live may dictate what pet you have.

What you need

Pictures of farm animals (optional).

Activity

Talk about pets that are often owned by children who live on farms or in the country. You could show the children pictures of animals such as a lamb, goat, piglet or pony. Suggest why some children could own such pets and some could not. Discuss why it may not be practical to keep a pig in a flat.

Extension

Invite a mobile farm to come into the playgroup or nursery class. (You may have to fund-raise for this.) They will bring some of the more 'portable' farm pets. The children may be able to stroke and handle the animals.

Talk about

Talk about the names for baby animals: kid / goat, lamb / sheep, etc, and the names for males and females: billy / nanny, ram / ewe.

Working pets

What children should learn

Knowledge and understanding of the world – to know how some animals that are pets can also help human beings.

What you need

The friendly local owner/handler of a 'working pet', such as a police dog, hearing dog for the deaf, guide dog for the blind, sheepdog, puppy walker, petting dog used in hospitals and old peoples' homes. (Ensure that it is safe for the animal to be handled by the children.)

Activity

Ask the owner/handler to come in and talk very briefly about his animal. Ask questions and encourage the children to do likewise. What sort of things does the animal do? What does it like to do best? How was it trained? Take especial care of children who may be afraid of the animal.

Extension

The children could colour pictures of the animal(s). Send the pictures, together with a group 'thank you' card, to the owner/handler.

Talk about

Talk about pets that help us and the jobs they do: police dogs; rescue dogs of all kinds, such as those who search in earthquake-damage zones for people who may be trapped; mountain rescue dogs; hearing and guide dogs who help individual people with specific needs. Do people have cats that help them?

Making a snail

What children should learn

Knowledge and understanding of the world – to develop cutting and manipulative skills and to select and use a mark-making tool to make a pattern.

What you need

Snails or pictures of snails; magnifying glass; thin card (A4) ruled into 3 cm strips lengthways; scissors; pens, pencils, crayons and chalks; sticky tape; thin straws.

Activity

Encourage the children to look through the magnifying glass at the colours and patterns on the snails' shells before they start. Help them to cut along the ruled line to make their own strip (or pre-cut if necessary). The children should choose from the tools available what they would like to use to colour their snail and then colour both sides. Demonstrate how to roll up about three-quarters of one end of the strip to form the snail's shell, then help the child(ren) to do same.

Prepare small bits of tape to fix on the underside to keep shell shape. Bend the remaining end up, draw on the eyes and stick on two short strips of straw for the antennae.

Extension

Have a snail race. Tie a piece of strong thread or thin wool to the front underside of each snail. Wrap the other end of the thread/wool round a pencil. Line the snails up and get the children to turn the pencil round in order to reel in their snail.

Talk about

Can a snail climb or go along anything? What might not be suitable and why? Does it take longer for the snail to go up something, or is it quicker for it on the way down?

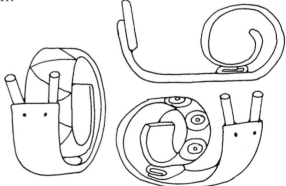

Snailarium

What children should learn

Knowledge and understanding of the world – to learn about snails and how to provide for and care for them.

What you need

A small collection of a range of snails (different sizes, colours, types); a clean fish tank (or something similar with a ventilated lid); garden soil; a patch of garden lawn turf; a bit of a branch, some medium size stones; a small box to collect snails in; some suitable snail food.

Activity

Discuss with children what they are going to make and what they will need. Gather the equipment together and prepare the tank (the new home) with the children's help. When all is ready, take small groups of children outside (two or three maximum with two adults) to look for snails. Each group should only select two or three snails. Look for suitable foods for the snails to eat and add these to the tank. Remind the children to wash their hands thoroughly after handling the equipment and the snails.

You will need to make sure the turf stays damp. Place the tank away from direct sunlight or radiators. After one or two weeks release the snails gently and carefully into the outdoors again. You could collect some new ones.

Extension

Look at the trails the snails leave on black paper and watch how they move either up the side of the snailarium or on clear plastic. Look at how they eat.

Talk about

What shape is the snail's shell? What does it feel like? Are all the snails you have found the same size? Are they all the same colour?

What gerbils eat

What children should learn

Knowledge and understanding of the world – to understand what gerbils eat.

What you need

Gerbil or photographs/pictures of gerbils; dry gerbil food (available from your pet shop); shallow containers; PVA glue; spreaders; broken-up cereal boxes, shirt-box card or similar (card is more suitable than paper for collages of a weighty nature).

Activity

This is a good activity to do if you have a group or class gerbil. If not, you will need pictures of gerbils for the children to observe. Look at the gerbil food. What does it look like? How do the gerbils eat it? What do their faces look like when they eat?

Let each child make a collage using the dry gerbil food.

Extension

Divide the card into quarters by ruling lines. The child can select different items from the food to put in each section.

Talk about

Do rabbits, hamsters and guinea pigs eat the same food as gerbils? Could cats and dogs eat the same food? What do all these animals drink?

Tropical fish mobiles

What children should learn

Knowledge and understanding of the world – the variety of colours and shapes of tropical fish.

What you need

Posters or books showing the variety and splendour of tropical fish; A5 sheets of white paper; coloured pens, crayons and pencils; scissors; fish templates (different shapes and sizes); sticky tape; strong thread or thin wool.

Activity

Show the children the posters and books of tropical fish. Discuss the different colours, sizes and shapes. Get each child to colour in completely his sheet of A5 paper, choosing his own colours, style, etc (he could colour both sides, but don't force him). When the sheet is all coloured in, the child chooses a fish template and draws round the template for as many fish as he can. Let the child cut out the fish, helping if necessary.

Extension

Turn one area of the room into a tropical water scene. Children could help to prepare the backdrop. Stick the fish on to a length of thread or wool and suspend them from the ceiling. Take the children in small groups on a visit to the local tropical fish shop/centre.

Talk about

Fish like to swim/stay in their own groups (shoals). Sometimes the shoals have hundreds of fish in them.

Creepy and crawly lotto

What children should learn

Knowledge and understanding of the world – about the features of some unusual and different pets.

What you need

Colour pictures of unusual pets – minibeasts, reptiles, etc (Tip: ask in specialist shops / centres for old copies of specialist magazines – you need two of each if possible!); paper; scissors; glue; A5 pieces of card; access to a colour photocopier; clear self-adhesive film. Sort and stick the pictures on to A5 sheets of paper in typical picture lotto style. Get two colour photocopies made of each sheet (not cheap, but worth it). Mount both colour photocopies of each set on to pieces of card. Cut up one sheet of each set into individual pictures. Cover both the game boards and the individual pictures with clear self-adhesive film.

Activity

With small groups of children (four maximum) play the lotto game. Encourage the children to look for distinguishing features, eg different skin colours, shapes, sizes, their different bodies, legs, feet, etc.

Extension

Take the children on a trip to a local pet shop that keeps unusual pets or ask if they could bring in some of the unusual pets for the children to see and maybe handle.

Talk about

What food do these animals eat? How do they move? Where do they live?